not thin enough

A Collection of Poems by
misty hicks

Copyright © 2021 Misty Hicks

All rights reserved.

This book, or parts thereof, may not be reproduced in any form or by any means without written permission from the author, except for brief passages for purposes of reviews. For more information, contact the author at mistyhicks3883@gmail.com.

ISBN 978-0-578-94976-5

Cover design and inside layout: Chris Boyer

Printed in the United States of America

Table of Contents

I Can't Eat It 5
Disgusted 6
An Apology To My Home 7
I'm Your Disease 9
The Lies She Told 11
Rising From The Sink 13
My Not Addiction 16
Restriction 18
The Monster Inside Of My Body 19
The Animal Renting Space Within My Body 20
Anorexia 22
Enemy In My Head 24
I Wonder… 30
The Journey Ahead 31
Sinking 33
An Apple A Day 35
Friday Morning 36
Red Tape 39
Forgive Me, Body 41
My Recovery 43
I Deserve More 44
Happiness Will Come 47
Being Skinny 50
My Fear 52
All Of My Senses Working Against Me 55

Many Days I Have Feared	57
Is Eating Worth It?	59
Battle To Win The War	62
I Don't Need It	64
Please Let Me Be Normal	67
The Girl On The Inside	68
Addicted	70
Puppet	72
Trapped	75
Ana & Mia	77
ABC Diet	79
Consumed By Unconsumption	81
Silly Girl	83
Running On Empty	85
Put Pen To Paper	87
Toilet Bowls Don't Hug Back	89
Today	90
Perfectly Unperfect	92
Not Thin Enough	94
Mindless Muncher	96
Delicate	97
Monsters Under The Bed	100
My Existence	102
Weight Of Words	103
Running For My Life	104
What I Saw	106
Counting The Calories, Secretly Loving	108
Society's Chameleon	110
Counting Calories	112
Purge	114

Paper Thin Masterpiece	115
What No One Tells You	116
I Know How It Feels	117
Take A Look At Me	119
Listen With Your Heart	122
The Curve Ball	123
Hiding From Bulimia	125
Revenge	127
Stigma Of Eating Disorders	129
Leave Me At Perfection	131
An Open Letter To Anorexia	132
The Scale	136
Just One Job...May Change My Life	137
I'm Just Tired	138
When I Go To Find Myself, I Know Where I'll Be	142
Skinny, Pretty, Dead	146
The Beast Behind The Beauty	147
Approval	149
About The Author	150

I Can't Eat It

The food is all around.
I can't eat it.
They are watching.
They will call me fat.
I refuse to eat,
At least here.
Too many people
Watching, staring.
I need to be alone.
Alone at last,
I feast….
Pizza,
Salad,
And pop…
Something with lots of carbonation,
It tasted good, but I need to do something.
Run to the bathroom.
Turn on the sink alone.
Up it all comes.
You wonder why I won't eat,
I pick at my food,
And why I have lost so much weight…
Yet I see me as
Fat…
A pig.

Disgusted

As I am standing here
Looking at the mirror
Which portrays an image of a girl.
I look at this girl in the mirror,
I look at her and say
"Who is this girl staring back at me?"
This girl is sad, disgusted, ashamed, confused, tired.
Sad that everyone around her
won't listen to what she has to say.
Disgusted with how she looks short, very thick.
Ashamed people would make fun of her weight
as if it's a joke.
"Fat."
"Ouch" that really hurts.
But yet she incense on shrugging it off
and crying every night.
Confused about who or what she should look like
to the public's eye.
Tired of always being made fun of
for someone else's sake.
That's what I see in the mirror
that portrays that image of that girl.

An Apology To My Home

Dear Body,

I am so sorry I almost don't know where to begin. I have put you through so much. And I hate to say it, but I'm going to put you through more as I try to fight this. And I will fight this.

All you have ever done is try to support me.

To my belly, you smile with warmth when you are nourished. But I've denied you that warmth countless times. I've damaged you and I've left you in pain. I know you'll never be quite the same.

To my legs, you carry me everywhere I need to go. When I eat, I strengthen you. I've forced you into weakness time and time again. I've risked breaking you when you are what bears me up.

To my voice, you are so soft and beautiful. You speak kindness, you sing worship to my almighty God. I've silenced you and made you weak. I've risked losing your sweet sound.

To my heart, the very one that keeps me alive and breathing. I've slowed you down and I've sped you up. You just want to keep beating. I've risked tiring you out. I've risked harming your strong and powerful beat.

To my liver, you are hepatic now. I've enlarged you to almost twice the size you should be. You just want to do what God has made you to do and cleanse my body. I've risked damaging you forever and putting you into liver failure.

To my bones, you are the very ones that hold me together. All you want to do is be strong for me. I've broken you down. I have risked osteoporosis and have caused degenerative bone disease.

But your forgiveness is abundant. It is evident as you accept the love I am working so hard to give you. Little by little, you accept the warmth of food, belly. Little by little, you are growing strong, legs. Little by little, your ring is coming back, voice. Beat by beat, you relax and rest, heart. Little by little, we begin to cope with your diagnosis, liver. And little by little, i give you vitamin D, bones.

I want to be your friend. I'm learning to appreciate you again, learning to fall back in love with you. I see how much you've done for me, how you would do anything to keep me upright. I no longer want to dwindle you. You are my body, my home.

I'm Your Disease

Sucked like a vacuum, I held my fear,
built up anger you want to hold near.

Shaking and trembling is what I feel,
purging my thoughts is how I heal.

Feelings of emptiness that have no depth.
Disappointment climbs the walls inside my chest.

You've lied to me all these years,
holding in the pain that has caused so many tears.

You think you're strong, but I make you weak.
I know the truth you're looking to seek.

You thought you had control over me all these years.
I'm your friend when you looked into your mirror.

You think you can forget me and run and hide.
I'm the only one that has stuck by your side.

I've given you comfort and relief.
Why now do you treat me like a thief?

I've stolen from you your sense of pride,
not letting you see that you're beautiful on the inside.

I've come to steal your strength and health.
Don't look to me to give you wealth.

You've been fighting this battle all alone.
Haven't you figured it out
you can't do this on your own?

This has been our secret for so long.
Do you have the courage to make you strong?

I'm the monster you won't admit,
afraid that now you'll have to commit.

The Lies She Told

When she smiles and laughs,
It no longer sounds hollow,
For she has learned
To mask her sorrow.
She's so uncertain
Of why she is sad.
Her life is fine now.
Why does it hurt so bad?
Tears won't fall.
She forgot how to cry.
Most of the time
She just wants to die.
She's obsessed with this concept
That skinny is perfect.
She pukes if she eats
Just trying to feel worth it.
She looks in the mirror
And hates what she sees.
She slices her skin
Screaming, "I don't want to be me!"
But by tomorrow
No one will know
She'll smile and laugh.
The scars won't show.
They think she is better.
They couldn't be more wrong.
She plays the part well,

They think she is strong.
Now and again
Someone sees past her mask.
They study her face
And quietly ask.
She looks back smiling
And she says, "I'm fine,"
But the sad truth is
She always lies.

Rising From The Sink

Crippling waves of anxiety smash against the side of the boat.
Broken pieces of the sailing structure fall away
in to the boundless space of the sea.
The current is rough, and I realize
I have chosen a destructive path.

I look around at my deck.
It is empty and I stand aboard unaided,
Which means I must face the tide alone.

Trying to steer the ship into prosperous waters
proves to be a task, and the fatal path has begun
to take a grasp on my mind.

My body trembles with unease,
the great force of the waves throws me across the deck.
There is no one to help me and no one to save me.
Do people want to see me fail, or they just not care?
There must be a reason for my loneliness aboard the vessel.

Infected with self-hatred
and no idea how to steer my ship away,
I see no choice but to expel my sustenance.
Drooping my head overboard,
I look down at the desolateness of the ocean.
The ship has left my control, and it begins to lose restraint.
At this point, I do not care;

I do not know how to lead it into calm waters.
I close my eyes and begin to purge over the side of the boat,
And the vessel speeds into the storms.

With one hand, I grip the sides of the boat;
I do not want to fall in.
Although it is unsteady, my ship feels safer
Than the openness of the vast ocean.
With the other, I forcefully retch
to abolish the goodness from myself,
Hopeful that it will teach me
to navigate my boat into buoyant tides.

I should be animated with panic, yet this is nothing new.
The supreme waves begin to rip apart the boat,
And I am knocked from my feet,
Left cast down on the floor.
I know I want to get up and prevent the destruction,
But my stomach throbs,
My watered eyes are blurred,
And my mind tells me to stay knocked down.

Disturbingly, the reckless waves and
Frantic storms have become my reality.
And then I feel the ship begin to descend
in to the great mouth of the sea.

As the water fills up the deck
and the waves smash down onto my person,
I rise from the hard, wooden ground of the deck.

I sprint down the sinking ship,
with the edge of the boat in my sight.
And I fall many times along the way.
However, once again I rise with the open water in sight.
Taking a leap of faith, I dive into the sea.

The fresh water feels beautiful on my damaged skin.
As I open my eyes in the ocean,
I see no wreckage or sign of the destruction of my boat.
Swimming up the surface,
I feel the beaming sun on my body,
And I enjoy the warmth and comfort it gives me.
I turn onto my back among the calm waves and shut my eyes,
But I can still see the bright sun above me in the sky.

I have cracked, but I will not be broken.
I do not fear falling because I do not fear living.
The deeper I sink, the higher I rise.

My Not Addiction

It's not an addiction,
It's really not.
But that mirror,
It's a source of affliction.

Not so long ago,
I could look in that mirror
And see nothing wrong at all,
But now I've got nothing to show.

The pressure to be perfect,
It tears away at my body.
At first it looked like nothing,
But it had a side effect.

I wanted to be one of them,
One of those girls everyone envied.
But the price to pay was my body,
Not a small pretty diamond gem.

It was never enough,
No matter what I did.
The skipped meals,
Turned my image rough.

But will it ever be worth it?
I stare and ask myself.

My image in the mirror,
Kept begging just to quit.

It became a nightly thing,
Standing on that scale.
And I was pleased to see
That the pounds kept dropping.

My hair was starting to thin.
My bones began to show.
Everything was different.
The desire was starting to win.

The pain I was putting myself through,
The constant suffering,
Everything was just a blur,
But nobody ever knew.

I try not to starve anymore,
But I could if I wanted to.
It's a big part of my life,
Now I'm trying to close that door.

It's not an addiction,
Really, it's not.
But that mirror,
It's a source of affliction.

Restriction

When I was thirteen I started to starve myself,
Hoping I could then accept myself,
But with all the weight I dropped,
The burning self-hate never stopped.

Restricting, crying, jumping jacks,
Searching for starvation hacks.
The number would drop day by day,
But in the mirror the fat would stay.

I got scared of my reflection
On my lookout for perfection.
Everyone was scared for me.
Couldn't understand what I would see
When I saw my body grow
In spite of what the scale would show.

I would purge a slice of apple,
Trying to fight my silent battle.
All I felt was sharp despair.
When I ran, I gasped for air.
Everyone was telling lies,
Seeing me through real eyes.

A vicious cycle owns my mind,
Telling lies that makes me blind.

The Monster Inside
Of My Body

Dear Monster inside of me,

I remember the day you showed your face to me.
Telling me I was ugly and worthless while destroying the inside of me. I never knew I wasn't worth much until you said it everyday.
Made me sincerely believe it so I agreed with what you'd say.

Since I was thirteen you have been telling me these things.
Started when I was on the playground, just playing on the swings.
Not letting a day go by without you reminding me.
Lost sight of who I was meant to be.
Friends and family started noticing the long trips to the bathroom after I ate.

Forced me into therapy which I never thought was that great.
I was given the ultimatum, kill you or not go to school.
Ever since then, I haven't stopped fighting, I will overrule.
The days go by and I see you shrinking, however,
I know you will always be a part of me,
so here's what I'm thinking...
I do what I can to shield you out,
Enough so that I can barely hear you when you shout.
I continue my life without the fear of you in it,
And I will survive without you making me quit.

The Animal Renting Space Within My Body

Your appetite for the absence of nourishment
Is far too great for me to feed
Your thirst for hollowness
Is too great for me to quench.

I hear you groaning in my stomach
Reminding me that the ache that I feel now
Is the fraction of the intensity
Of the bliss I will feel
Once you're finished with me.

But only if I obey
I starve for the day I find myself dressed in bones
Elegant
Lovely
And beautiful

This dream is what I float into each night
When my gut howls in torment
Pleading for grace
But its howls are silent
Compared to the cravings of my mind; of you.

My animal
I would give anything to bite off a piece of your ego
And snicker as you watch me swallow it whole.

Your eyes would widen
At the realization that I'm brimful enough
To up and leave you-
Leaving you with nothing.

For you are nothing without me
And without my body
That day will come.

Until that day, I'll let you shove your finger
Down my throat
I'll let you cackle at the number on the scale.

I'll let you lick the mouth watering tears
Off my face but know-
This will end.
And when it ends,
I will come for you.

Anorexia

Please, please, please, leave me alone.
I am begging you to please leave me alone.
You have convinced me that I am not worthy
of love and stability.

You have taken away my sense of self worth and joy.
You have torn me from my friends and stolen
what was supposed to be the best years of my life.

Living with you has made my mind a battlefield.
Every single minute is filled with conflicts
between you and my healthy self.
I try to argue with you,
but I keep ending up losing the battle.

Logically, I find myself in a continuous state of distress
but you convince me that I am nothing without you.
You have made me believe that I am disgusting and fat.
When the truth is,
no matter how much weight I gain or lose,
no matter what dress or waist size I wear,
you will never be satisfied
and keep telling me the same thing.
It feels like I've been taken hostage
by an evil dictator who now controls my every move,
every thought, choice, and action.
I didn't see it coming; it started slowly.

Your voice in my head,
I slave tirelessly to abide by your rules.
My brain became fixated on food,
on my body, my movement,
my life revolves around these things now.
But now is my time to take my life back
and that means kicking you out of my life.
So leave. Leave now and never come back
I don't need you and I never did.

This is goodbye.

Enemy In My Head

There is this "girl," she was my friend,
She lives inside my head,
She started off so friendly,
So caring and so kind.

She helped me just to function,
To cope with everything in life,
She helped to make me "better,"
Perfection she would help me strive.

There is this "girl," she was my friend,
From the world she kept me safe,
She told me how to live my life,
And helped me to be brave.

She made me feel quite "special,"
A better person I would be,
She stopped me from feeling lonely;
The world against her and me.

She promised she could help me,
Make people like me more,
But, how she could do that,
I really was unsure.

She said if I was skinny,
People would like me,

She told me if I was skinny,
My flaws they would not see.

The less and less I ate,
The better she'd make me feel,
She told me to keep going;
That this was the only way to heal.

All my trust I put in her,
As my pain began to fade away,
Listening to her every command,
With the promise, I would be okay.

She, became my best friend,
My secret from everyone,
I felt so strong, so powerful,
Like against the world I had won.

But without me even noticing,
The kind voice in my head,
Was no longer my best friend,
She now wanted me dead.

As the pounds fell off me,
The more she'd call me fat,
Screaming obscenities at me,
From my head where she sat.

The promise of having more friends,
Quickly faded away,

As she made me totally isolate,
The promise gone, that I would be okay.

Without me even knowing,
She'd dug her vicious claws in me,
Showing me all her many flaws,
How disgusting and fat I was, she made me see.

And no matter how hard I tried,
Nothing I could do was right,
From my friend, she became my enemy,
And I could see no end in sight.

The calm voice turned to screaming,
And she'd twist anything people said,
The voice that started as my savior,
Now made me wish that I was dead.

And if I tried to fight her,
She'd inflict more pain on me,
Quickly I started to realize,
From her, I never would be free.
Such an evil monster,
That started off so kind,
As my own mind turned against me,
To the truth she made me blind.

Clinging on, to control my life,
But the most ironic thing of all,
Was I had lost total control,

And I was now backed into a wall.

The thing that was meant to save me;
To get me through, keep me alive,
I believed she was really helping,
Yet I was starving to survive.

Physically and mentally,
I deteriorated very quick,
Although I couldn't see it happening,
I became very, very sick.

But once the denial had faded,
And the reality started to sink in,
I knew that I had given up,
And that she would finally win.

My only way of surviving,
Had turned its back on me,
The voice I once saw as my friend,
I now wish I could be free.

I'd look into the mirror,
And the truth I could not see,
She'd warped my mind and vision,
She had total control over me.

She'd say people were lying,
That only she was right,
As people would try and help me,

Against them I would fight.

But the war was in my own head,
Not against the world around,
And as I began to accept this,
My own voice I slowly found.

And now I've grown to hate her,
The voice I once saw as my friend,
She never tried to save me,
She wanted my life to end.

And while she served a purpose,
Starting as that sweet voice in my head,
She turned into a monster,
And became my enemy instead.

Walking On Eggshells

Walking on eggshells, what does that mean?
You're living with a part of me no one else has ever seen.
The eating disorder has come to take over me.
The vomiting only I ever see.

What can you do to help me you ask.
Do you say something to me?
What questions do you ask?
The wrong words, the right words,
come out of your mouth.

Trying to keep calm but wanting to shout.

Will the words you say make it better or worse?
There's no right or wrong with this eating disorder curse.
So you walk on eggshells doing your best.
Trying to say and do the right thing,
it's a bit of a test.
You're too fat or you're too thin
are words that accidentally come out.

But it's not these words that eating disorders are about.
It's a control thing,
comfort self-harm all rolled into one.
So we're all walking on eggshells before too long.

Understanding, caring, empathy,
help is a way out.
Talking to others who have been there
is what it's all about.
We can take comfort in others
who have been in this place.

Then when we walk on eggshells
we can do it with grace.

I Wonder…

I wonder…
I wonder who I would be,
Were I not what I am now.

I wonder who I would be
Or whether I would know
Who I am at all.

I wonder if I would be
What I fear most.

I wonder if I would be
What I hope for most.

Not set back in my track,
But moving forward.

Life takes its course
And we steer the wheel.
But we cannot control the engine-
That is in God's hands.
How did I get where I am now?

'I wonder' came about from me contemplating
Who or what I might be had I not embarked
Upon the journey of Anorexia and Bulimia.

The Journey Ahead

A journey lies ahead of me,
I can travel it, step back, or remain;
I must do half the toiling,
I must embark upon some pain.

But there's pleasure from that journey,
For light shines on the path-
A hope, a future, happiness,
Reason to smile and laugh.

The choice is mine to make it,
Only I can make that move;
Help is there to guide me,
Counsel, advise and soothe.

Yet the path is hard to conquer,
The journey a struggle and fight;
Yet I know that at the outcome
I encounter happiness and 'light'.

If I remain I will go backwards,
For there is no standing still,
For sliding down is all that happens
If you don't push up a muddy hill.

The decision I can't quite make yet,
I must consider how I might cope;

I need assurance, courage, honesty
Before I am to take the steps
and live my hope!

'The Journey Ahead' tells peaks something
Of the decision I made to recover from Anorexia
And Bulimia and what this might entail.

Sinking

I hate the very thought of fat,
But only on myself.

On others, weight can suit them,
Be part of them,
And I love them.
But I hate it on myself.

This causes me to sink low;
I was already down,
But now I sink even lower down.

The trap of the sinking sand,
Drawing me deeper.
Until all I survive on is hope.
Even my dream fades away.

I feel so alone.
And trapped.
Like a caged animal;
Knowing that when free,
I can run,
I can run free;
Roam free and be with the others.
Yet as it is,
The bars hold me in;
Limiting my space and movement,

Some pass by:
"How beautiful!" they exclaim.
Others reckon I am better off held in,
Yet they complain at my raging behind the bars.

Lioness behind bars;
Yet I don't bite.
I'm simply trapped and alone.
Longing to be free.

―――

'Sinking' tells of how I would sink into
Feeling more low when I examine my body
And body size in my desire for the 'perfect body.'

An Apple A Day

An apple a day to
Keep me healthy you say,
Just make sure it's organic,
And have two a day.
You only said one,
But better be sure,
Blend into a juice,
Pulse until 'pure'.
Healthy is the goal in sight,
Avoid the cookies and candy with all your might.
Those family meals too, wave goodbye,
For you'll steam your meals,
With no oil you can fry.
Celebration drinks are off the cards,
Friends mean food,
An edible junkyard,
I am on a diet,
The concerns made quiet,
Congratulations, well done,
With each pound lost,
One by one.
No junk a day,
No matter the cost.

Friday Morning

A Friday morning,
At the crack of dawn.
Step onto the scales,
Keep in the yawn.

A Friday morning,
It's the dreaded day.
I do not want to know,
How much I weigh.

A Friday morning,
The burden of the scale,
Afraid, alone,
Tucked in is my tail.

A Friday morning,
I am so ashamed.
The weights jotted down,
By a nurse unnamed.

A Friday morning,
Is too much to bear.
Will I weigh less,
If I cut my hair?

A Friday morning,
The dreaded day.

Today I found out, the burden I weigh.
To Whom It May Concern

To whom it may concern,
every day I try to look cheerier.

To whom it may concern,
but I cannot look at myself in the mirror.

To whom it may concern,
I am not pretty.

To whom it may concern,
I really do not want pity.

To whom it may concern,
some people call me fat.

To whom it may concern,
now I wish my stomach was flat.

To whom it may concern,
sometimes I starve myself all day.

To whom it may concern,
emptiness makes the pain go away.

To whom it may concern,
I count the calories to be burned.
To whom it may concern,

I've taken laxatives and pills to lose weight.

To whom it may concern,
I am filled with so much self-hate.

To whom it may concern,
I was able to eat all three meals today.

To whom it may concern,
but I had to purge it away.

To whom it may concern,
I think I am not human, but a problem.

To whom it may concern,
with purging, all the bad thoughts
and memories are forgotten.

To whom it may concern,
my thoughts continue to worsen.

To whom it may concern,
so much, I do not feel like a person.

To whom it may concern, I wish I was dead.
To whom it may concern,
only then, the thoughts will get out of my head.

I am sorry if I caused you to be disturbed,
But it would be nice if I could know to whom it may concern.

Red Tape

Back, belly, thighs, wrists.
Which path do I start with?

I take my red tape and wrap my arm up,
Then my legs, I'm about to throw up.

The mirror cannot be correct,
I object to these attributes I have!

"Mad, mad." Is all I cry.
When I'm really sad, mad.
Sad about my body.
Mad about how I can't change the image of it.

This picture-perfect human
has too much red tape wrapped around her thighs.
What's with the red tape?
Well red tape, when you read into it,
Communicates insecurities only one person sees.
As maturity builds so does unreasonable things.

So next time you see red tape
wrapped around your home town,
take it off. Peal it, pinch it, demand it come off.

Because red tape isn't healthy to start a fashion trend with.
And to the eighty-six deaths caused by Anorexia per year

alone.

I'm sorry you had no place to go home to in your brain.
Pain is beautiful and it's crucial to live.
So just do that for a minute more. ..
LIVE.

Nobody is perfect and no brain is too small.
That's how much I care for you.
If you needed guts I'd give them all.

Forgive Me, Body

I extend my deepest apologies to you.
From the degradation you have suffered
since age thirteen,

To the current behaviors that sicken your strength.
I have harmed you.

Your hips match the curves of every planet,
So why do I treat you as anything less than otherworldly?

I open you up,
And let hurt seep into your grounded soul,
Never caring about the memories I'll leave on your skin.

I threaten your inner working systems,
The gears in you will only fit together for so long,

And I push you to your limits,
Risking all you have brought me up to be.

Forgive me, body,
You didn't deserve a host who treated you as the enemy.

The battles I have fought in your bones
were something you should have never had to prepare for,
But thank you for being ready.

Thank you for not letting me down in my sea of insulin,
Thank you for not letting me get stuck
in my quicksand of pills.

You have kept me alive longer than I ever
Thought I would live and I am grateful.

But body, still forgive me.

For not seeing the stars in your freckles,
The universe in your eyes,
The places you will go in your feet,
And the hope in your hands.

You have been with me forever,
So I vow to fight for your forgiveness,
And to prove I believe in your worth.

My Recovery

It will be challenging.
It will also be worth it.
You will relapse, and that's okay.
(as long as you keep fighting.)
You may feel alone in your struggle.
You will help others who are struggling.
Your loved one may not understand,
But you can always explain.
You will have good days, and bad days,
But the bad days will get fewer.
Your problems won't magically go away.
But they will be manageable.
You might not feel different at first,
But when you're done you will be:
Happier,
Healthier,
Stronger,
And recovered.
That's why you have to keep fighting.

I Deserve More

I want to start off by thanking you. Thank you for being a friend of mine. A best friend. More than that, my other half. For making me feel safe. For helping me go from uncomfortable to comfortable. Thank you for helping me get through the darkest of times.
You made the pain stop and I love you for it.

You are there for me all day, everyday. If I need you to burn down an emotion or comfort me in a crabby situation, you always know, and you are always there. When I spend time with you, nothing else matters. I don't have to worry about not being good enough for you.

I never feel crazy about telling you something that is pushing my buttons because in the end, you'd wipe out those furious feelings with numbness. It is awesome. I love it. I don't care that you made me disgusting. And, I especially don't care that you won't let me tell anyone about you. I don't care because you are giving me everything I need so I'm doing my part and staying loyal. I know no one will understand me the way you do. Unfortunately, no one does. That's why you're my other half.

I hate to admit it, but you don't only serve me, but you hurt me. I still want you, but we both know that the time spent with each other comes with a high price. I've tried to break up with you numerous times, don't you remember? I've had

enough of you because I am enough. I made the decision to move on and let go of you. This will be a difficult transition, but I am committed to end our abusive relationship.
I may fall for your voices and rely on the temporary numbness you give me at times, but I'm not giving up the fight till I become more powerful than you. I'm fighting for a life without you. I'm fighting to be free of your demands. I'm fighting because I deserve more than you offer me. I deserve more than the voices shouting in my head when I've made a mistake. I deserve more than falling onto you for a quick escape when I've had a bad day.

I deserve more than stuffing my feelings down. I deserve more than killing my insides by following you into the bathroom because you'd whispered into my ear that I had eaten too much. Or because you would whisper that I need to "release" my emotions by a purge. Love- sick, that's all you offered me. And hell, I am valid to feel all emotions; including the bad so I am able to feel the good.

That's right, happiness in which you would never approve me to experience yet, you would manipulate me that I would be my happiest if I engaged in our "bad romance" together. That disturbing cycle you peer- pressure me into doing-- purge, restrict, repeat. Sure, it satisfied my needs in the moment. But in the long run, you made me feel tired, weak, and unmotivated.

You tell me from time-to-time how I'll be more attractive if I stick by your side. But physically, you actually made my liver enlarged, given me gum disease, weakened my heart, and hair fall out. I know I will be faced with your tempting words trying to capture my heart again, but as I'm learning more about my true and beautiful self, your voice will slowly mute as my strength and ability to choose a full life will heighten.

Happiness Will Come

Dear Anorexia and Bulimia,

That's right, I'm calling you out! Hear your name loud and clear. This is my notice letter. I am done with you, I'm tossing you out! Pack your things and leave. My body's a temple and you are no longer welcomed here. My conscience is clear and I'm finally picking up the shards of my life, the ones you left in a shattered mess on the floor. I'm cleaning up these broken pieces while finally scraping away the days wasted, the countless hours spent lying on the bathroom floor; door locked, water running, heart pounding, just you and I. Here is where you began to teach me your rituals. Here I went even after I had scraped all the butter off my bread just as you said and bounced my legs up and down, like the sporadic pattern of popcorn kernels as they dance over the heat. My legs imitated the popcorn I wasn't allowed to have, let alone touch to my lips. These sacrifices were not nearly enough, more had to be done to reach the unattainable goal. These are the truths I was too blind to see, these are the sick things you have done to me.

You made me the kind of person I never imagined I'd be. You made me lie to the ones I love and because of you, I grew even more detached from myself. Slowly but surely everything else faded so easily into the distance. You were now placed front and center. "Come to me, I will guide you. I will fix you. Do just as I say and one day, you too can become hollow, pure, and positively holy", you whispered.

Purity and holiness I still lacked, but hollow I was, as I barely made it through school no thanks to you. My head spinning, breathing deep, stomach pain, I'm keeled over, but I'm "just fine". Always "fine", you made me utter along with the sad excuses for my quiet rumbling abyss of a stomach. What I did manage to eat, you made me "get rid" of almost immediately as if I was going to inflate right then and there. The food my mother so lovingly prepared was quickly expelled of and all was blamed on the fabrications of my state. "That'll be an order of numbing endorphins with a big heaping side of shame coming right up, ha ha get it? Coming up." Instead you fed me with little chants and motivations, "nothing tastes as good as skinny feels," "the girl who skips dinner wakes up thinner," "you are not a dog, don't reward yourself with food."

You led me to a point that, when threatened with a hospital bracelet, I smiled at the mere challenge. How sickening, other people must've thought. They were undoubtedly right, I was sick. I looked in the mirror, drowning in my own thoughts and skin, staring glazed eyed at the mess I was in, a single tear and a faded grin, I was overwhelmed at the sight of my skin. I was plenty smart, but I had just googled how many calories were in gum, toothpaste, Advil even.

What have you done to me? What it truly was, no one would have believed. I had become a ghost of my former self, a mere shadow of the happy, go lucky girl I was. All for what? Thin? All for the looks, the whispers, the compliments… was it really worth it? Somehow I thought it was as I lost my hair, my humor fleeted, and the smile that everyone loved so dearly up and disappeared. But I was skinny, right? Dying? Maybe. Happy? Hardly. "When I am skinny, happiness will come."

Funny how that played out, or in fact didn't.

Being Skinny

Being skinny…
I thought I knew about being skinny
After all, the media showed me
Pictures of Tyra Banks in all of her
Callipygian glory with her twenty four inch waist

But no one told me the story behind
Her pristine, pouting face
No one told me all the unrealistic expectations
And the realizations that come when
You're standing on that scale and the numbers-

The reds, the blues, the greens all of them screams
And when you begin to listen to the voices
You hear their promises and pain grows in your eyes
As you make more choices that seal your fate
And ignore the fact that they are lies
And that you are hungry
But hunger is pain and beauty is pain,
So they're the same, right?

No!
And I learned this the hard way
Just thirteen, I emptied my stomach because I was empty inside
Because it was far easier for me to hide
Behind this mask of "no thanks, I'm not hungry"

And yet I realized
There was nothing for me to save
This was taking me to my grave
And I would never be happy with myself
If I kept doing this to myself
Nothing will become clearer from looking in the mirror
Examining every flaw on my body
Because everyone has flaws
And the more I focused on myself and my problems
And listen to the voices in my head
I would shut everyone else out until I was dead

But I'm too young to die
So I thought about it
I decided it wasn't worth it
Why say "is it worth the calories"
When I should be saying
Is it worth sacrificing everything-
My family, my friends, my life
Just to be this nonexistent thing

Being skinny

My Fear

Some people have a fear of heights.
I have some friends with a phobia of clowns.
Others of mice, the dark, spiders, and flying.

Me? I have a fear of the numbers that stare back
At me from the thing I dread having to step on.
The thing that has traumatized me since I was thirteen.
You see the scale and I have a long history
With more lows than there were ever highs.
And I have never known what it has felt like
Not to prepare for the same lecture
And to get the same disappointing sigh from my father
And to leave the doctors office with a feeling of dread
And embarrassment when I look in the mirror.
I am reminded of the thing I hate the most.
When I brush my teeth, when I tie my hair back
I am reminded.
When I am given clothes as a gift knowing the gift receipt is in the bag "just in case" I am reminded.
When I go into the store to return what was in the bag pretending to look for something in my size
and inevitably never finding it because I am inside a Hollister where all the thin pretty girls are looking at me like an elephant who has invaded the territory of the gazelles wondering why she has lost her way to the watering hole, I am reminded.

When I finally told someone how I felt they told me
"Well maybe you should eat less." So I did.
I ate less, and less, and less, and less.
Until water bottles started to replace meals.
Sleep started to replace hunger.
Until distractions became my favorite past time.
Until my body started to register that eating food is bad and being hungry is even worse.
When I feel like I'm about to give in
I remind myself of the times I have cried in the dressing room when something my size didn't fit.
When I see someone wearing the same outfit as me except it looks better on them.
It always looks better on them.

Over time it gets easier.
You learn to accept that you are just a black hole and that is collapsing into itself getting smaller and smaller by the second.
Except you aren't getting smaller just yet but you have the hope and knowledge that you will.
Because you are finally in control of something in your life.
Because you have the power to make sure it goes your way and stays that way.
You also miss food.
As surprising as that thought might be to yourself it does come around more often then you'd think.
It's draining when you have to make up an excuse to not eat tonight's dinner.
Or getting out of plans with friends for the fear of them

getting hungry, which you know they will.
I hope one day I can be as happy and confident with myself like the girl that sits on the far end of my Sunday school class.

All Of My Senses Working Against Me

Touch…
I glide my fingertips over my thighs.
I feel where my skin had once stretched.
I've lost ten pounds this month.
But is it worth it?

Sight…
I look into the mirror,
Society has projected self hatred onto me.
I feel like a child's alphabet mat with foam cut out letters.
I am the letter G crammed into the cutout for letter C.
But is it worth it?

Smell…
I don't like to leave my house for dinner.
Maybe, if I avoid the smell of nutrition's temptation
I can be skinnier.
But is it worth it?

Taste…
I am hungry.
I haven't had a full meal in four days.
I eat a packet of almonds for dinner.
That should hold me over.
But is it worth it?

Hearing…
Speaking out loud.
I falsely assure myself
"One hundred more calories for the day!"
"Just have some water."
But is it worth it?

I have withered away into nothing.
But that's the goal, right?
My brain screams at me to snap out of it.
I can't continue like this.
I gradually practice self care.
Day by day,
I welcome the numbers with open arms.
It means I am providing my body with what it needs.
I am worth it.

Many Days I Have Feared

Many days I have feared.
Many days I have feared.
Feared a store front.
A car window.
A still pool of water.
A click and a flash.

Many days I have feared.
Who looks back at me.
My reflection haunts my heart.
Saddened by the monster I see.
Tiny crinkled eyes.
Fat thighs.
I'm starting to lie.

Many days I have feared.
Who will find out about me?
Will my throat begin to bleed?
When will somebody help me?

The day I feared has come.
My head hangs low.
Her cries echo in my head.
"Andrea I promise, never again."
My heart feels like lead.
One day I fear.
What will she say?

Can she take this pain away?
I tell her my thoughts.
My words hang in the air.
The hurt lifts away, leaving me there.
One day I look to the sky.
I think it's time to fly.
The sun.
The breeze.
The earth.
I finally feel alive.

Many days I smile.
With my reflection, I am starting to reconcile.
My heart feels full for the first time in quite a while.

Everyday I look in the mirror.
Everyday I look in the mirror.
Because I am beautiful.
I am strong.
I am brave.
And now I am no longer afraid.

Is Eating Worth It?

Feeling guilty while you're eating, when your hunger is like breathing when your lungs need oxygen.

You listen to the demons in your head.

They ask you if it is worth eating that?

They ask you are you sure you want to eat at all?
I mean look at you, you could skip a few meals.

You start believing them. You skip your breakfast first, then your lunch, then your dinner.

You start drinking one to two cups of warm water to fill you up and one to two cups of cold water to lose the weight.

You eventually don't eat for a whole day, then two whole days.

Then three but when you hit the third day you pass out, your body is starving.

You say you're not hungry every time people talk about food.
It's always you're not hungry.
But in reality, you're so hungry.

You want to eat but when you even look at the food that demon steps in...remember you need to skip those meals. You want to be like everyone else, right?

You continue to tell yourself fat last longer than flavor. You tell yourself it's for your own good. You tell yourself skip dinner wake up thinner, skip lunch lose a bunch, skip breakfast go on a fast.

You tell yourself you want the flat stomach and thigh gap. They told me to love myself. So I stopped eating.

You always think to yourself everyone else is:
Better
Prettier
Skinnier
Smarter
Funnier
And happier than me.

The fourth day...after getting four hours of restless sleep because you're so weak and dizzy and your head hurts so badly from the lack of nutrients in your system that you physically cannot go back to sleep until you've eaten something and continue to maintain the same body weight, size, shape as you did the night before, coupled with a dose of self-hatred.

You go to eat and again that demon comes back
and tells you–you can't possibly eat.
You can't possibly gain weight, grow in size,
change your shape you have longed and worked for.
It tells you think before you eat.

So you just stop eating.

You stop trying.

You stop caring.

You stop breathing.

Battle To Win The War

Her soul was hungry for change,
But her mind was made up to stay,
So her soul was left to starve,
Her mind in a power-hungry craze.

Nothing distracts her mind from the numbers,
She's addicted counting and subtracting,
Her spirit locked in the box of getting smaller,
Pain lying dormant, waiting.

At once, the box too small to sustain her,
Her captive soul works hard to break through,
Slowly but surely getting stronger,
Finding the will to make her mind something new.

Months of battles and talking through strategy,
Mind and soul are nearly to level ground,
Farther from the beginning than the end,
But falling seems so safe and sound.

As she looks at life as she knew it,
And life right there before her eyes,
To her soul there is no question,
She knows what she has to decide.

So the battle gets bloodier and bloodier,
It gets harder and harder to walk through that door,

But five years later she thanks her past soul,
Each small battle won the war.

I Don't Need It

Pick it up.
Put it down.
Move it to one side.
Move it to the other side.
Swirl it around
like the endless thoughts that consume your mind,
Preventing you from doing just that.
Consuming.

But whatever you do don't swallow.

Pretend that you've already eaten.
Pretend that drinking water will fill up the void that's feasting on your fears.
The void that's getting bigger, as you get smaller.
Pretend that the thoughts going on in your head
can fill the emptiness inside.

Pretend that the screams in your mind, filling the gaps where knowledge should be,
Are leading you to be a better version of yourself.
A slimmer version of yourself.

Don't look at it, don't think about it, don't talk about it.
Don't touch it, don't think about touching it,
Don't tell anyone that you're not touching it.
Don't taste it, and don't smell it,

Or you'll remember what it's like to be satisfied.
Don't listen to people telling you to eat because the voices
In your head are loud enough already.
If you don't think about what you're missing,
You don't need it, right?

Wanting and needing are two separate entities;
There's the want to conform and distort your body into an
unreachable ideal,
There's the need to feel better,
There's the want to never have to feed your body and be able
To ignore your mind trying to combat itself.
There's the want to never need again.

Except now you know that you need it.
Now you know that there's no reason to fear the things
That you need to stay alive.
That what you see in the mirror doesn't reflect your reality
And that your reality shouldn't be scared of becoming a
Stronger version of itself.
A version that is self-nurtured and not scared of
Replacing the screams with words of affirmation.
Now you know that a love for the things that keep you alive
Doesn't mean you're diminishing your self worth.
Because the only thing doing that was the fear of the
Mirrors reflections and the idea that one day
you could love to eat again.
The fear that more food meant less love
because society paints a slim picture with
Invisible realities.

Now you are mesmerized by the outline of your hips
And the amazing ways that your body can move.

Now you know that life is more
than a series of numbers on a scale,
Or distorted pictures of a sad reality
morphed by societal expectations.

Now you know how to lock away and burn all the thoughts
That once ignited your dismay.

Now you're free.

Please Let Me Be Normal

Please,
Just for one morning
Let me keep down my food.

Please,
Even for one morning
Let me look in the mirror
And tell myself I'm beautiful.

Please,
When I get to church
Let the smiles I give
Be truly happy.

Please,
After years of holding on
Let me forget
All of the memories
And the pain that accompanies them.

Please,
Stay out of my world
Let me continue on my path
To making my world safe again.

Please,
For once in my life, let me be normal.

The Girl On The Inside

I feel her.
After every meal, every snack,
every traitorous look at anything sweet.
Sometimes she can get too angry.
Her hand reaching up and grabbing mine.
Her screams escaping along with my lunch that day.
I just ate one cookie, "I'm sorry"
but her voice pounds in my head.
Was that necessary?!
The only thing you gained was pounds, don't you see?!
You disgusting creature, do you not know of self control?
But both of us know the answer to that.
Although I hate her, I am thankful for her.
Another way out, ya know.
It's okay to eat this dessert now,
for it will no longer be with me tomorrow.
I tell myself it's just until I lose ten pounds, then I can stop.
Fifteen pounds later I realize stopping was never an option
she won't let me.
I hate her.
At least she is honest though.
She shows me the truth about myself,
What no one else has the heart to tell me.
Sometimes I can see her in the mirror.
She is a shaky little girl, wild eyes, blonde hair.
I feel her cold hands as she grabs the extra skin that barely
lays over my jeans.

This will be gone soon, I promise, she assures me.
I almost got rid of her once.
I told my friends my problems and went and got help.
I was so close, so close.
But it wasn't until she had trapped me in my closet with the goodbye video freshly made
The tears drowning my confidence.
And the bottle of expired pills downstairs.
But she saved me.
Her voice coxed me to sleep.
That's when I realized I will never get rid of her.
Not as long as I want to value my life.
So we made a deal.
I stay alive and so does she.

Addicted

In a matter of days, I have become addicted to letting go.
Letting go of the food that my mouth consumed only hours before.
The smell of vomit filling my nose like gasoline it burns.
I know it's wrong, but I cannot escape a feeling so intense.
The way that my toothbrush penetrates my throat,
The way my throat clenches in the absence of air.
I am a sinner, forcing harm onto myself,
but my body screams out of necessity.
A drug. An addiction.
Sometimes I make myself vomit
even when there is nothing to.
Spit piles up in my mouth, I hate myself.

Daddy once said,
"Pretty girls are skinny girls."
When I became skinny, I was told I was beautiful.
Telling myself in between gags, that this,
this is how it's supposed to be.

When the skinny girl gets skinnier, it's a disease.
When the big girl gets skinny, it's a miracle.
My dad said he was proud of me.

When people told me I was sick, I told them they didn't know the difference between sick and struggling.
Convinced of the notion that pretty people are skinny people.

I look at my reflection in the clear toilet bowl water,
I do not recognize the girl that stares back.
She is broken, bare.
Some may say that she is beautiful,
She is skinny.

Puppet

Trigger warning: rape, self-harm, mental illness, eating disorder.

I have always been your doll.
You've always just sat there and watched me fall.
Fall into you, again and again.
If it's ever going to stop, I don't know when.

With your strings on my soul, you pull on my heart.
Why do you live to tear me apart?
I don't even know who you are.
A million faces, but you never go far.

You were the man I thought was my love.
Responded to my "no" with a trust and a shove.
You whispered sweet nothings into my ear.
But they were simply nothing, just what I wanted to hear.

You turned love to a weapon and affection to a gun.
I was just so broken I didn't know I should run.
Each sweet word became a bomb and you were a minefield.
The pain you caused will never stop, never yield.

Because you stole a part of me I'll never get back.
Took it so swift, without a trail to track.
You took my innocence, you took my pride.
You took everything I was, my childhood died.

You were the voice that I thought was a gift.
You came without warning and your destruction was swift.
Eat less, eat less, until you're left without fuel.
I couldn't disobey, I heeded each command, each rule.

My body is a prison, my broken mind the guard.
In mountainous ribs, my heart was barred.
Each bone became a prisoner, trying to escape through skin.
Each pound, each calorie, a battle I couldn't win.

You weaponized insecurity, and fed on my pain.
What do you want?
What do you hope to gain from the destruction of a thirteen-year-old girl?
Or making a sixteen-year-old make herself hurl.

You were the thoughts that always wished me dead.
When I listened to each demand and followed what she said.
Turning middle school tools to ways you suppressed me.
But everyone blames the person, the thoughts they'll never see.

How do you fight back against your own mind?
Without destroying yourself, death seemed so kind,
You had an alliance with the reaper and you kept up his supply.
It's so unfair, just leaves me screaming "why?"

Why would you take a happy, kind teen
And turn her to such darkness that she has never seen?

Why turn her skin to canvas and her blade to a brush?
And when anyone offered help, you made her hush.

I still don't know who or what you are.
So many faces, each left their scar:
In flashback memories during day
and nightmares during sleep.
In days broken down, too exhausted to weep.

I have marks on my arms, scars of a battle I can't win.
You broke my spirit so I broke my skin.
What else to do when you're falling apart?
No weapons to fight back against the virus in your heart.

How do you kill a virus without killing the host?
How do you battle something visible as a ghost?
How hard is it to battle your own mind?
How to break you down when we're so intertwined?

Trapped

I am trapped inside my body.
The shell of a girl who cries at the thought
of breakfast, lunch, and dinner.
Or the days when I say "forget it" and eat how I should.
Just to be punished by someone screaming
in the back of my mind.
That I'm not good enough,
That I don't deserve three meals, or two, or even one.

The days where I eat enough for a week
and wonder why I don't lose weight.
So I'll starve myself.
But my desire to be skinny is often unmatched by my desire
to have that split second satisfaction of chewing food
and actually swallowing it.
Then begins the ritual of turning on the shower or the sink.
Something to drown out the sounds of my desperate attempts
To rid my body of its fuel
in hopes to never feel my thighs rubbing together,
Even though that was a feeling that never bothered me
Until those other "Ana's" and "Mia's" said it should.
The hydration epidemic seems like a Godsend, in a world of
Cystic acne and Instagram models that all say the same
things, that water cures all.
You have so many excuses for why you must drink two liters
everyday,
Not that anyone knows that's your caloric intake for the day.

"It's good for your skin" I smile, sipping cold water to get that beautiful feeling of pure,
Clear nothingness pouring into an empty cavern.

Spewing lies learned from the Internet becomes a regular practice
"I'm not hungry"
"I'm allergic"
"I'm vegan"
Anything to get them to leave you alone.
God, "Why is everyone so obsessed with food?"
I'll mutter to myself while searching for the amount of calories in a teaspoon of rice.

Ana & Mia

In April of 1996, I met Ana and Mia. They promised me that they could make me beautiful. That I could be skinny, just like those cover girls. That I could have anything my heart desired. They promised that they could make me perfect. So, true to their word, they made me skinny, sort of. I went running and dieted. I made goals for sit ups and mile points. I worked myself to exhaustion and ended everyday on the scale with a measuring tape in my hand. I recorded my weight loss, and physical accomplishments. I cut lunch out of my daily routine, and for the first time someone noticed a difference. I was "fading" as they put it. I had stopped eating, smiling, and talking, and started purging. I spent breaks crying on the bathroom, and I wanted to die.

They, Ana and Mia, followed me everywhere, accompanying me to meals and to the bathroom afterwards where I puked up what I had eaten. They closely monitored my behavior, and eating habits, and forced me to lie at doctors appointments. To lie to my friends. To put on a fake smile everyday, and the cuts they so carefully carved on my wrists and to say "I'm fine". But fine is just another word for broken, another way to scream for help without making a sound. A plea for someone to look me in the eye and say no you are not! It is just another hopeless attempt to communicate that I feel hopeless, helpless, and worthless. It is my dying attempt to say that I am as far from okay as I can get.

But instead of saying these things, I just smile and say, "I'm fine" because Ana's and Mia's nails are digging into my wrist, telling me it's time to step away from those around me, they don't want me anyways, just get out. So, I get out. I leave, because sometimes that's what you have to do. Sometimes you just have to get up and leave everyone, and everything behind. But no matter how far I go, no matter how fast I run, no matter how much I laugh, and write, and read, and live, they're always there. They shadow me, watching me like a hawk, whispering in my ear, don't eat that. Do you want to be fat? You are disgusting. You should be ashamed of yourself. And when I give in, when I let them inside my head. I stop again. I stop eating. I stop hoping. I stop living. And here I am, I've stopped again. And because of you, BECAUSE OF YOU ANA AND MIA, all I want is to disappear. It's not that I want to die, but if I didn't wake up in the morning that would be perfectly fine by me.

I am trying to scream out for help. But your cold hands are clamped over my mouth, keeping my screams confined to my mouth, to my head, and to my mind. I am confined to my mind, and I'm tearing myself apart. Why won't you let me out? I want to get out of here. I need to get out of here. Ana and Mia, please, your welcome is worn out, now leave. LEAVE NOW. I can't keep doing this. I can't keep pulling myself down and apart. Please, just let me go, before I fall apart.

ABC Diet

Water,
Low-calorie, no-calorie, sugar-free and...water.
When I only ate a bite of my lunch and threw the rest away
you didn't notice.
And you didn't notice how I always went to the bathroom
straight after eating, either.
Of course, you didn't follow me,
so you couldn't have heard my tears hit the floor
as I told myself to push my toothbrush
just a little farther down my throat.
Choking as my sanity came up and flushing it
down the toilet.
Washing my mouth out, careful not to swallow
the extra calories
That might be lurking in the tap water like demons.

Trying diets I had found on the Internet.
Sneaking food into the trash when you weren't looking.
Eating in front of a mirror.
Crying over a bathroom scale,
Cause I only felt pretty when I was hungry.
Constantly attempting the ABC diet.
300 calories the first day, 300 calories the second day,
200 calories, 150, 100, 100, 50, 200, fast.
Ana was my best friend.
Along with her sister Mia.
Reminding me how fat and ugly I look in every mirror

Or pane of glass I so much as glanced at.
Promising that life would be better when I'm thin.
And I believed them.
150, 200, 400, 350, 250, 200, fast.

Some people say they don't remember the first time they chose not to eat.
I do.
I remember looking at the food on my plate
and telling myself I wouldn't eat because I wanted to be pretty.
200, 100, fast.
I lost 5 pounds, then 10, then 20. Striving to be double digits and not triple.
I was so focused on becoming the shape
I was supposed to be.
"Nothing tastes as great as skinny feels," I would tell myself,
Twisting and turning in the mirror, sucking in my stomach.
250, 200, 150, 100, 50, 100, 200, 200, 300, 100, fast.
I told you about my eating disorder,
But you shook your head and rolled your eyes and told me
To shut up because I didn't look anorexic.
250, 100, 50, fast.
Fighting a daily battle,
trying to convince myself it is just an apple,
Not 95 calories, thirteen hours without food, 75 sit ups.
Trying to reprogram my brain to be normal.
500, 400, 350, 300, 250, 200, 150, 100, 50, fast.
Am I pretty yet?

Consumed By Unconsumption

Can't see it, can't have it, can't taste it,
Or you will surpass your limit.
Don't let your body throw a fit.
In the end, you know that it's worth it.
Take your eyes off the prey,
Turn and run away.
It's tempting, but do not submit.

But the sizzling sauce is tantalizing,
And the roasted beef is appetizing.
The luscious aroma is mesmerizing,
And what you had is not satisfying.
Though, you must ignore,
Or you'll want it more,
Even though this habit is agonizing.

People are asking what's wrong.
They wonder why you are not strong.
Will the comments prolong?
They swallow you all day long.
But you go and hide,
Keep your feelings inside,
And hope that they move along.

You are beginning to grow weak.
You have no energy to speak.
You can barely mutter a squeak,

But you still have things to critique.
Don't get in your head,
Ignore what's been said,
You don't want to end up dead.

People have figured you out.
You are consumed with self doubt.
You wonder if you should back out
And seek an alternate route.
You are out of control
And stuck in a hole,
But you don't want to get out.

Your vision has gone black.
Your bones are about to crack.
Your habits are off track.
Death is waiting to attack.
But you don't die
And you realize why.
It's time for you to come back.

Now you have goals to meet
That your friend helped you beat.
You finally feel complete.
Listen to your heartbeat.
You have survived.
You've been revived,
Because you began to eat.

Silly Girl

While she once found comfort in pain,
She now finds consolation in pleasure.
Funny how it happens that way.
Silly girl, she was.
Telling herself she was full when all her body had
Consumed was the muscle of its withering heart.
Counting. 50, 30, 80. Enough.
Loopy girl, she was.
Eating more than she ought to
When she lent herself the privilege.
Preparing. Drink the water.
Senseless girl, she was.
Tying back her long brown hair,
While she still had hair to hold onto.
Bracing. Hold on.
Mad girl, she was.
Tickling the back of her throat
Like her grandmother tickled her infant tummy.
Breathing. Don't forget to inhale.
Insane girl, she was.
Throwing all sorts of foolish things in the alluring white ring.
Crying. Tears of sadness. Tears of success.
Deranged girl, she was.
Hurling her life away.
Sitting in a puddle of shame. Ready to make a change.

9,125 days of hurt.
Days of rest.
Days of growth.
Days of recovery.
She is better.
Smiling in the euphoric sensation of self-liberation.

Running On Empty

Hate never silenced her words
And compliments never brought about change
All she ever did was purge
But her mind remained tainted and strange
Different from the others
Yes, it's what she had planned
That reaching out attempts were smothered
So she could not make a stand
She will make her perfect
Or so she taught her to believe
That calories and a flat stomach
Would make her worth something
Diet pills here, laxatives taken there
And soon a stomach grumbling meant cheering
200 calories was the limit, anymore she would not dare
For fears that her peers would be watching and jeering
Her parents worried, her siblings cried
But nothing could stop her, not even herself
She was ready to be skinny, not care if she died
For no one could ever understand how she could be helped
It wasn't until a long time after
When she realized who the enemy truly was
And fought for her happiness and laughter

The girl who was thought to be lost
In the end, she made it and stopped listening
To the negative evil side
And finally started living
No longer afraid and no longer cried

Put Pen To Paper

Anorexia and Bulimia.
Battles of the mind. Battles of the body.
It all describes the same struggles.
It was the diseases that landed me in the hospital.
Therapy of all kinds was scheduled.
Art, music, family, group, and writing.
Writing. A way of describing the demons
in a way everyone could relate.

Look right, look left, write here, write there,
breathe in, and breathe out.
Put pen to paper and just write. Write.
Writing is a way to release the tension
buried deep within me.

No one wanted to be the one to admit
we were being suffocated,
But, writing is a way to break
from the grasp around my neck.
That big black hole had already swallowed most of me.
Don't eat that. Don't sit. Don't drink that.
You don't deserve to be happy. You don't deserve to live.
You deserve to die.

Look right, look left, write here, write there, breathe in, and
breathe out.
Put pen to paper and just write. Write.

Writing is my cry for help from the slow death I am in.
Vocalizing my thoughts means I receive help to
Combat the specific errors in thinking.
I'm not writing poems because it's a required therapy,
I am writing poems to save my life.
Because when you put pen to paper and just write,
It is a way to escape my disease and search for life.

Toilet Bowls Don't Hug Back

Don't romanticize this and say some boy or girl will pick you up off the floor and hold you in his arms and wipe your tears away and kissing you anyways. This is the gruesome reality of always smelling like puke. It never goes away. You will get it on your clothes, you will get it in your hair, it will be everywhere possible. Want toilet water splashed into your face? Then oh boy you'll love this. How about bleeding knuckles and scratched up throats from your nails and teeth. Giant puffy cheeks because you throw up so often your glands stay swollen. Running to purge in dirty public bathrooms because you found out your waitress gave you regular coke instead of diet. You will have to deal with the stares when you start disappearing after meals. Your mind will go crazy you will feel like a prisoner, you are a prisoner. You will never feel more alone in your life and the sound of your gagging will be the only remembrance of that day. As that is all you will do. Hug people not toilet bowls. How about not even being able to eat a couple of carrots without throwing up because that is what this will come to. It won't come to daintiness or frailness and to be light as a feather. It will come to scars and poison and a burden on your mind heavier than anything imaginable. Soon you won't know how to digest food. It will come right back up. This will destroy your life. Crying on the floor gasping for air as you can hardly catch your breath and tasting the food that was once in your stomach. But now is not. This is the gruesome reality. Don't you dare call it a lifestyle.

Today

Today…
Today I started up the set of sixteen stairs it takes to get to my apartment,
But I was too weak so I stopped at the sixth step,
Sat down, and caught my breath.
How many days had it been?

Today…
Today I tried to open the door at the end of the hallway,
But my arms weren't strong enough
And I had to put my entire body against the door.
How many days had it been?

Today…
Today I saw my dad for the first time in three weeks and he hugged me.
His arms, they doubled around my entire torso
And he asked if I had lost weight.
How many days had it been?

Today…
Today I sat at the table staring at my hands.
And they asked, when was the last time you ate?
And I was too scared to tell them.
I didn't know how many days it had been.

Today…

Today I skipped my counseling appointment because I
couldn't get out of bed.
My bones frail and thin, how could things get this bad?
I raised up my shirt, fat I thought.
How many more days until I am thin?

Today…
Today I willed myself to get up with a strong feeling that I
Could look in the mirror seeing what I wanted,
But I still saw swollen masses of skin
And heard all the awful names he would call me.
So, I put on sweats and a hoodie
hoping in a few more days, I will be thin.

Today…
Today I woke up in a hospital bed with white all around.
Three IV's with a sodium drip, antibiotics, and morphine.
Questions were asked.
Oh no how many days had it been?

Today…
Today they brought you to me as if they knew
I needed you all along.
You said "hi, mom" and today was the best I've ever experienced.
Today…
Today I ate my food and didn't stop in front of the mirror.
I'm trying because in my head I always knew
being loved doesn't equal being thin.

Perfectly Unperfect

Oxford dictionary defines "perfect" as having all the required or desirable elements, qualities, or characteristics; as good as it is possible to be. But the words faint and dry on my mouth as a result of the sadness provided by it. Words defined by humans, humans who dare to find perfection…But cannot find themselves.

And I would look at my friends just to see that our eyes disagree,
But our mouths shout "skinny," "pretty," "perfect" I wanna be.
But we agree on what perfection means and whisper to our minds that we do not fulfill. Locked in our prison, covered by thoughts, thinking that the world does not deserve us,
But the world does not deserve perfection either.

And let the word burn my skin, see the powder of my segmentation turned into dust. Mixed with the tears that my eyes cried.
And I would look at myself in the mirror to say that I wasn't beautiful, and to define what beauty means as the own word says "be" but we are not.

And if your body is a shell that suffocates your soul and makes your heart smaller, answer to the fresh air on our naked cheeks touched by God's tears. But if we do not define perfection, are we good enough to think as a good thing? Are we good enough to think what it means and it's as perfect as a finger to a ring?

But the butterflies are dead,
And their black and white wings float on my heart.
Accompanying the loneliness of what it feels not to fulfill a place.

What if the place is my heart?...
What if I don't belong here?

But where is here?
The comfort of warmness of another soul by my side,
Saying that I fulfill a definition written by a man,
Put down on a book and thought by women.

And I do not know what this definition means or what it brings,
But teach me how to be enough for the enough.
And teach me how to breathe with broken lungs in this short sharp oxygen earth.
And if makeup covers what we do not want to show
I hope that makeup shadows my wishes,
My deep wishes of how it would be to be perfect.

Not Thin Enough

Anorexia and Bulimia have become my entire life for twenty five solid, miserable years. Every month I'd stop eating until they took me to the hospital, then when I got home, I'd do it again. Every month I'd drop around ten pounds, some months I'd drop twenty. At 5' 2" when my weight dipped below ninety five they decided I had an issue. I was put in the hospital and the first thing I did was complete a 100 question survey. Simple questions about my sleeping patterns, my depression, self-harm, suicidal thoughts, and of course my eating habits. When these questions about food came around, I got very uncomfortable, but the nurses didn't really seem to notice. They asked me if I knew why I was in the hospital. I said "no." They tried to explain that I had an eating disorder and wasn't getting enough nutrients. They obviously didn't understand. I told them I had an eating problem since the age of thirteen and that if I wasn't brought in earlier, there's no reason for me to be here now. Do you know what they told me? They said, and I quote, "You weren't thin enough."

This is a doctor we're talking about. A doctor with a PhD told me this. I realized then that I knew more about eating disorders than the doctors did because they are not something you can just learn about and understand them. You have to experience it to understand it. Anorexia and Bulimia are about the way you see yourself. Anorexia and Bulimia is body dimorphism. Anorexia and Bulimia are not a weight or a number. Anorexia and Bulimia is not being able to look at an item of food without the number of calories immediately popping into your mind. Anorexia and Bulimia are voices in your head constantly telling you not to eat, constantly telling you how fat and pathetic you are. It is a mind crushing, body crippling disorder and will ruin your life and don't you dare tell me it's just a number. Because some cancers have a higher survival rate than eating disorders. Because there's more people with eating disorders than people with green eyes. Because eating disorders have the highest mortality rate out of any psychiatric illness, largely due to heart failure and suicide. It's not a 'lifestyle', it's not a 'diet', it's not 'just a phase' and it's absolutely not just a weight measurement.

Mindless Muncher

I am a product of comforting hugs, gut wrenching laughter, and humbleness.
I am a product of societies harsh views on bodies, self image, and self worth.
I am a mindless muncher, professional purger, and a caloric chess master.
The creation of another part of me, a distorted and contorted image of myself that I struggle with every single day.
But with that comes inner strength.
A strength that has glittered within me for as long as I have been on American soil.
I will take the good times and the bad times with gusto.
Because I know every experience is like an ingredient to this incredible recipe, of who I am today.
And today I am someone who throws out as many who hugs, who tries to never leave the house without laughter, who tries-and sometimes fails- to be humble.
I am also someone who bleeds strength, who promotes love and determination.
To the very core.
But more importantly I am recovering, I am a survivor.

Delicate

I equate my relationship with food to a magic act. Move the food around my plate, take a bite, spit it in my napkin. Tada! It's gone. Magical, right? Inside I praise myself for giving the illusion that I am fine, just fine, while also rejoicing that I did not give into the sin of food sliding across my tongue and into my stomach where it makes me grow big and distorted. How can I be the girl in the vanishing box if I don't even fit in the box?

My whole life has been about finding love. Feeling it from someone else and most of all not feeling it towards myself. Ugly. Fat. Muffin top. Thunder thighs. Words attacked me, sticking to my senses, numbing them to the beauty that I could have been. I wanted to be described as delicate. Characterized by a fine structure or thin lines. I figured out in middle school, that the best way to be slight and slender was to simply not eat. The thread count of my sheets was more than my caloric intake and I found that the more that I grew in, the more people took notice. A stranger came up to me in the store filled my basket with rice cakes, salad, and water and told me that I was beautiful. That day I put the rice cakes back. I had never been beautiful. Funny, that when I started killing myself was when I finally felt alive and loved.
At night when I lay in bed, my fingers played a tune over the hills of my ribs to which I plotted out how to eat less the next day, all the while chanting less is more. Less is more. Like the wings of a bird who was too weak to fly my shoulder blades

popped like wings trying to break through the delicate skin of my back. There it is again, delicate. Such a pretty word used to describe pretty people. When I was freezing in the 100 degree heat of August, I felt that I could still lose that last ten pounds. When the bones of my spine began to peek out and I began to bruise from hugs, I felt I had finally achieved the definition of the word. Adjective. Requiring careful handling; not to be rudely or hastily dealt with.

Despite the pleadings from Andrea, Ana and Mia became my best friends. They taught me how to perform magic. Make the food disappear through slight of hand. I know my disorder hurts her, but it's too hard to talk about my desire to disappear and achieve delicateness so my apologies are disguised as gifts. Go to lunch: I'm sorry I threw up your lunch. Movies: I'm sorry I spend all my energy resisting and purging food and I'm too tired to go out with you. Gifts: I'm sorry you have to spend your time watching me die. We argue. I must eat, I'm so frail. I don't like that word she uses to describe me. Frail is weak and sick. And I wish to be neither. I long to be called delicate, like a beautiful butterfly that is held up by thin wings. She says I had a beautiful figure once and I know she just wants me to be healthy. Health makes me cry and I do not want a figure, of any kind. And I know her version of beauty is internal and that I don't need to starve from my hips and thighs.

I spend hours staring at images of women whose bones show through their skin. I thought it was the most beautiful thing. I found truth in sayings such as "nothing tastes as good as skinny feels." I need these images, this "thinspiration", because I can't envision a world were I can inspire anyone while my thighs rubbed together. My desire for connectivity and support is fueled by these images of women just like me striving for perfection, aiming to be delicate.

When you're a young woman and you feel like the connecting point is through the hatred or the shame that you have around your body, that becomes so dangerous. The hunger for love is so much more difficult to remove than the hunger for bread. I've learned that it's easier to grow in and believe that you will never live up to the "thigh gap" and hollow bodies of those portrayed as epitomes of beauty, then it is to grow out and to love yourself while looking in the mirror that society says shows the most important part of you. We are taught to love what we are not. We are taught to aim for a goal that requires killing ourselves to achieve it. And I hope I survive long enough to learn the most important lesson: There is so much that tastes better than skinny feels.

Monsters Under The Bed

My little sister meant the world to me.
When she was ten years old she loved her pets,
playing dress up, and cooking.
Oh how she loved to cook.
She would make a delicious dish out of anything.
It killed me that I could never taste it.

That's got to be the worst part of having an eating disorder.
Not the cold chills, or the yellow nails, not even the occasional hunger pangs from when I did screw up and eat.

The worst part was that my sister never got to have me taste her "super-choco-tastic" cookies.
The worst part was not being able to go run
and play with her.
The absolute worst part was having to hear her pray at night that I don't die, and seeing her cry during my ever-so-frequent doctors visits.

There was always one thing I could look forward to, though.
When we got home and she was all settled in bed, I would check her room for monsters.

In the closet, behind the door, under the bed, everywhere.
She didn't believe in monsters anymore, but I've always done it, and we always got a kick out of it.

That's why when she had whimpered that she saw a monster under her bed I was surprised.

One of the most admirable things about my little sister was that she was so brave, so seeing her that way came as a shock. I checked under the bed, and realized she was right, there was a monster under that bed.

It was staring me right in the face...and that's why I've always hated mirrors.

My Existence

What is my purpose in this world?
To take up space, to be a filler in an empty place?
The idea of existence has always been confusing,
Am I here to succeed?
Or will I end up losing?
But to me there has always been something ahead.
I'm trying to reach my goals, proving ambition isn't dead.
So far I am pleased with what I have done.
My life is not easy, but I believe I have won.
There was a time when I was like all the rest,
But I realized I can't dwell on the past,
It will just leave an empty space in my chest.
So I travel on through every difficult day.
Knowing that happiness is never too far away.
What is my purpose in this world?
I may not know yet.
But I'm sure I'll find out, the farther I get.

Weight Of Words

I used to look fat, but thanks to my parents- I lost my weight.
But, now the weight that over flew through my mind and made me hate myself the most.
Hate myself that I didn't even lose weight the right way…
I lost it by losing it- losing my mind.
Parents telling me to eat smaller portions,
Which only led me to even smaller portions.
Parents telling me to go outside and run,
Which led me to fainting for eating those small portions.
Parents telling me to eat bigger portions to regain my weight,
Which led them to speaking to me about "dropping a few pounds."
Parents telling me that I need to look decent for them,
Which led me to ambiguous thoughts.
Thoughts that no fifteen-year-old girl should think.
Thoughts that no boy or girl should think.
Thoughts that no one should think.
Because at the end of the day, I hated myself more.
But, what I hated the most is the look of my parents face when they called me fat.
But, what was even worse was when I looked at the mirror and realized I only lost myself.

Running For My Life

There I was another day
Spent counting miles
Subtracting calories calculating deficits.
Run, run to look good, run to look pretty, run to lose weight.

Bracing the cold
One morning in February.

Opaque.

Alone on the trail.
Feeling the wind and the snow pierce my skin.
Feeling transparent as if the winds were going to claim me as their own.

I would tell people that it's normal
That I'm an avid runner.
My BMI?
Low, you say?
No.
More like, normal.
For a runner as good as me.

There I was
One sunny morning in the month of May
Crouched on the kitchen floor
Gripping the edge of the counter

Slamming cabinets refusing to get up.
Denying that I need help.
My body? It's fine.
Or so the voices said.

Now the voices are getting quieter.
Instead of you don't need that
I hear
Add some more of that
And
Another scoop of this.

Now when I run
It's not to reach a certain number
And not to look good in jeans.

I'm running from my demons.
Running for myself.
I'm running for my life.

What I Saw

Thanksgiving feast
Family gathered around the table
Smiles, laughter, love, joy
But what I saw…
Calories. Fat. Guilt. Humiliation.

Birthday party
Children running and playing
Happiness, presents, celebration
But what I saw…
Pizza. Cake. Hours at the gym.

My bathroom
Slumped over the toilet seat
Toothbrush down my throat
Excitement, pain, relief, shame
Because what I saw…
Thighs jiggling. Stomach protruding. Arms flapping.

My living room
Joslynn sitting across from me
Tears, confession, desperation
And what I saw…
A daughter who understood

One month later…
Getting dressed to go out

Looking at my body in the mirror
And soon I hope to see…
Beauty. Strength. Triumph.

Counting The Calories, Secretly Loving

Counting the calories,
Secretly loving each bite,
Is being skinny
Worth all this fight?
Seeing your hipbones?
Collarbones too?
Searching for a thigh gap,
Even though there's so much "you"?
Hating yourself
For eating an apple
When you really should be
Drinking a diet coke?
Being on the scale?
Of seeing your weight?
Look at the "perfect girls"
And wishing you hadn't ate?
Is it worth losing your hair
Clump by clump?
Running into something lightly
And leaving with a lump?
I know how you feel
I've been there, done that
And at the end of the day
I still felt fat.
I let words hurt me,
Scar me for life.

I let these words drive me.
I let society make me
Into something I'm not.
Now here's a lesson
I wish I'd been taught-
Starving yourself
Is never really right.
Trust me, it isn't
Worth all the fight.

Society's Chameleon

I'm custom-built to expectation
A situational chameleon
But no one knows,
Because what they see is only what I show them
I know it shouldn't be this much work,
Projecting an image of being "okay."

Be yourself, they tell me.

I can't be myself
Because that girl is a disaster.
She has anxiety attacks
She purges and restricts
She harms herself
She sinks into a depressive state
She's moody and destructive in her mind

People don't like that.

They prefer a projected image:
Put-together, cheerful, kind, and compassionate
No questions asked.
If I let down the mask,
I will let down everyone.

Numbers Consume Me.

Numbers, no I'm not talking about math or accounting or statistics I'm talking about life. By the time I was born my life was run by numbers; when I eat, when I nap. My life was a schedule and I did something every two or three hours. Milk at 6am nap at 8am and repeat.

Then as I got older I learned that I was defined by a number; my age, my grade.
People never asked me what I wanted to be but what grade I was making in a subject and how old I was.
Why not my aspirations instead?

As I became more intellectual my hobbies were ran by numbers; food consumed, time and speed.
No one asked me whether I liked running
they simply asked how fast is your mile?
No one asked when's your next match
but to me to put more fuel in my body.
Numbers, they became too suffocating; my weight, my height.
Sooner or later I realized I'm only a number.

No wonder other women are going through eating disorders. Life is about how much space I take up or what size clothing I can fit into. When will life be more about living than about numbers.

Counting Calories

A mind-game; fueled by the intense hatred
for my own biology.
Addictive, poisonous, destructive;
a path leading to my ultimate starvation.
My heart screams for sustenance, my brain is barely lucid.
Torture tactics planned out by my own demons.
They override my conscious.
Too self-conscious, afraid, to eat the calories?
"Skip a meal", the fat will melt away eventually.
How long until my skin hugs my ribs tightly
like two best friends?
This is the easiest option.
Ok-one bite; just enough
to help place one foot in front of the other.
Dinner time becomes math time.
Count, count, count. How high does it add up?
Heart pounding, stomach curling in on itself.
Sustenance, where's the sustenance?
It doesn't take long
before my body stops crying, whining, screaming.
Empty.
Counting calories was a game.
Not skinny! My jailers sneered. Keep counting!
But I escape. Took a pause. Even if only for a moment.
No more counting.

For once, my body fought back.
But I woke up this morning and my jailers are here now asking:
Want to play a game?

Purge

Consumed by the urge
There's no room for your words
There's no room for my thoughts
For rhyme or for reason
Time is immaterial
Come and goes in waves
Consummating this consumption
Hatred for my weak and worthless
Body, wind, the lack of will
Everyone can see what you have done
The cold is everywhere
Penetrating to the deepest layer
I shiver as I find
That only hell was left behind
Couldn't satisfy
Couldn't satiate
Maybe it'll work next time
You'll just have to wait
But it never works, you're never whole
The hole, it grows and grows and grows
In the end you'll wonder why
But all the debt was only mine

Paper Thin Masterpiece

"Treat me like glass, tear me to shreds like I'm paper."
She had said
She spoke harsh words,
but she whispered them like sweet nothings.
The monsters in my head.
Inhale, exhale.
The darkest days and the longest nights I lived in her world.
She danced along side me, painting scars like poetry.
The coldest war and the hardest battle
you were trapped inside me.
Beautiful, cold, fragile.
My paper thin masterpiece.

What No One Tells You

You hear them
Names in textbooks, thrown around
Anorexia, Bulimia, EDNOS
People don't understand
Why not eat? Food is yummy
It is not about food at all
It is a way to deal with life
To deal with the peer pressure,
The stress of wanting to be good enough and
Disordered eating, is not the way to go
No one tells you
What is going to happen
How a demon will get inside your mind
Torture you with thoughts of how ugly you are
Until you want to lay down and starve or run until 4am
Or obsessively count calories because you feel "fat."
Ana is not going to make you
Beautiful, smart, or skinnier,
She is going to steal away your happiness,
Your freedom, your friends, everyone who you care about
Whether it is Ana, or another disorder,
They make you choose
Them or life?

I Know How It Feels

I know how it feels
To hate the food you put in your mouth.
So, why not go without?
A day?
Barely eat anything?
Not a problem.
Because you can use it.
You need to lose that weight.

I know how it is
To avoid the prying questions, innocent at first.
What did you eat for breakfast?
Did you have anything to eat earlier?
You need a hamburger, okay?

I know how it feels
When the questions turn suspicious.
Are you eating?
How much do you weigh?
Do you know that I can see your bones?

I know how it is
To be more worried about body fat than nutrition.
A few more pounds.
A few more pounds.
I'll be skinnier=prettier.
I know that twisted pleasure to hear the doctors

Say you're under weight.
Yes, that's exactly what I want.

And I know how it feels
To get in too deep and lose yourself.
In the numbers of meals,
Numbers on the scale,
Numbers of the calories.

I know what it feels like
To be trapped in a body you believe
To be fat, ugly, and disgusting.

And I know what it feels like
To look back at pictures, years later,
And discover that a bag of bones
Is not what I wanted to look like.
That my body ate the muscle and the fat
Until I was hollow and haunted.
I was haunted.

Rise from the ashes, it can be done.
I know how it feels.

Take A Look At Me

Take a look at me
What do you see?
My body is hollow
I want to be free

Free from this curse
That keeps getting worse
When I look in the mirror
It won't be reversed

I keep resisting my food
I'm just not in the mood
To feel ugly and fat
See my stomach protrude?

I work out like crazy
And I'm never lazy
Must get rid of this weight
It hasn't been easy

I look at my face
And I want to erase
The roundness, the ugliness
Want to lose every trace

I watch on TV
I read magazines

And on every page
The bod of my dreams

I want to feel pretty
It's not enough to be witty
Folks only will love you
When you learn to look sexy

I wish my bones all sticked out
Too many to count
I'll quit when I'm skinny
If I could, I would shout

The frustration I feel
Becomes more and more real
When I look at myself
And I find no appeal

It isn't enough
It is never enough
I need to be beautiful
I have to stay tough

I'm fighting the pain
Pray I don't gain
Even one little pound
That would fill me with shame
I always feel weak
I feel guilt when I eat
I'm battling hunger

I can't look like a freak

People around me
Must be in a hurry
Cause they don't even stop
Don't bother to worry
As I waste away
Like a hollowed-out shell
Of the girl I once was
With my story to tell

Listen With Your Heart

Your eyes see that she's smiling,
Your ears hear his laughter.
Your mind tells you that they're okay,
But your heart tells you to look further.
Your eyes say that nothing is wrong,
And your ears hear her words.
But your mind is at battle with your heart
Because your heart can see the hurt.
Your mind deceives you
Into thinking she's okay.
But your heart can hear the quiet screams,
And see that his once blue sky is all of a sudden gray.
You try and shrug it off,
So you believe that everything is fine.
And in your heart you know it's not true,
While you're at ease in your mind.
Your eyes and ears will deceive you.
Best to ignore them from the start.
So don't listen with your ears, your mind, or your eyes;
Instead just listen with your heart.

The Curve Ball

It was always too hot or too cold in her troubled mind.
And no amount of tossing or turning could ever tucker her
out enough for her to tuck herself in,
At night her mind was a race car that never ran out of gas,

Running round and round on the same old track.

Replaying, the same old memories.

Reciting, the same old words.

The same words he used when he compared her
to her mother,
Who was thirty pounds lighter.
"Fat, fat, fat!"

Three letters that devoured every beautiful place
left in her mind.
Three letters they used to brand her, as if she
was the world's property.

Three letters she engraved onto her hips, so when denim
rubbed against raw skin she would remember to
skip dinner that night,
Because she was forced to believe that beautiful looked like
skin pulled tight over a hollow skeleton.
She thought she had to mold herself into the perfect cookie

cutter girl.
That beauty came in only one size:
Extra small
In one shape:
Thin

She took her definition of beautiful from Webster's
Dictionary for the Corrupted Society,
Because beauty was never about how much you weighed,
or the size of jeans you wore.
I used to be in the eye of the beholder,
And somewhere down the crooked line of humanity
that all changed.
Curvy was out and skeletons were in,
But darling you are the curve ball we are throwing at society.
You are the girl with the beautiful wide hips
and filling features,
You are the girl with the power to change the
course of history.
Ignore the scale and be the girl you were meant to be.

Hiding From Bulimia

In my closet
I'm sitting
I'm thinking
I'm crying
I'm restricting
I'm cringing
I'm crawling
In my closet
Balling,
Is me
This dying thing.

Calories
Calories
Calories
They rule my world
I can feel it beating inside I'm gonna hurl.
These thoughts
Spinning
Faster than the revolver of a gun,
Russian roulette with my life,
My fingers
My toothbrush
My knives
Drive the deep piercing my throat,
Hold it
Hold it

Make yourself choke
You think this is a joke?
I regurgitate my food, my meals, and those pills that kill
Regurgitate like how society throws in our face that we should be,
Those same girls that are so unhealthy because they are so called "beauty".
Keep going
Going until you're empty
Empty like those calories that fill me to the brim
Empty like the people who comment you need to be thin
Empty
Empty til nothing is there
Remember be lighter than air
Restricting, purging, starving
All this is barging into my life and I can't control.
I'm sick this is getting old.

Run
Hide
You poor, poor girl
You were never strong enough to grow in this world
Go
Now
Into your closet
Back where you started

Revenge

Yeah, you had me there for a while
You had me on-my knees
You took my glow and my pretty smile
It was my body but you had the keys
I felt completely dead back then
I couldn't even laugh
I pushed away my family and all my friends
Just so I could follow your path
You took my hand when I was weak
When I was lonely, tired, and lost
You whispered that you would help me
But at what cost?
Yes, I loved you for a bit
I believed all your lies
You made me feel like some hot stuff
I didn't even see the blindfold you slipped over my eyes
And by the time I could see what you'd done
I was your prisoner and you took me away
And you laughed as I turned into a skeleton
I tried to fight but you begged me to stay
Why did you choose me?
I wish we never met
And you know what I'm going to do now that I'm recovering?
I'm going to tell all your dirty secrets

You won't take anyone else under your spell
I'll make sure everyone knows what you really do
I'll make your world a living hell
Better watch out Ana and Mia, because I'm coming after you!

Stigma Of Eating Disorders

The media says that girl who sticks her fingers down her throat does it because she wants to lose a couple of pounds, when in reality she does it because she wants to get rid of all the pain inside that is torturing her from the outside. "I'm just sick", she says as she returns from the restroom. With her sore throat, raging like a burning fire in the esophagus, from the acid in her stomach that she so loathes, and wishes was concaved with her ribs glistening the surface of her skin. People think she's healthy. She is not emaciated. She looks fine. She is not fine. She is not okay. The outside is a materialistic representation of what each human is perceived as by the world. The inside speaks so much more, yet has no voice. No one can hear that this girl is dying on the inside. No one knows how deep the darkness goes in her soul. It is abyss of utter hell. It is the voices constantly barking at her, "YOU ARE FAT" "YOU ARE WORTHLESS" "YOU ARE NOTHING" 24/7, those voices speak and tatter at her self-esteem. She believes she is fat, and that she takes up too much space. Exercises for two hours each day to be the tiniest she can be, because she believes that if she is not the tiniest person on this earth, she is without purpose. She convinces herself that her presence is unnoticed, and if she were not there, not a single eye would flinch to look around and seek her out. "YOU ARE FAT." "YOU ARE WORTHLESS." "YOU ARE NOTHING." These words repeat over and over as she walks through the store, as the bustle of men laughing and rustling for phones in a black hole they call a pocket. When she walks down the street, crossing the road sticking to her role as a typical pedestrian. When she is at home, in front of a lifeless piece of glass that controls her, and as she picks and pulls her skin wishing unwanted parts would disappear. People can't hear these voices as they run through her brain, bashing every cell down just to take up space. They can't see the damage of her throat close to being ruptured, or the skipping beats of her heart. Since they don't see they just say, "she looks fine". Will they continue to say she is fine when she is laying in front of the porcelain bowl with no heart beat to record? Will they continue to say she is okay when she passes out from dehydration and not even a breath from another human being can't reawaken her lungs?

No, they wouldn't. They would run screaming, wishing there was something they could do. But they were too late. They didn't realize that it doesn't matter what you look like, what your weight is to have an eating disorder. They only saw the smile she faked and the false laughter she conveyed when she was actually sad and far from healthy. As people, we need to look and realize that anyone can struggle with an eating disorder. This girl wished people knew. She wished they could see that struggle so maybe she could be saved even when she didn't want to. An eating disorder doesn't have a specific face. But, it has the power to take away what a person is and what they can be. Stop putting a face on eating disorders. It can happen to anyone and anywhere.

Leave Me At Perfection

Leave me at perfection,
It's just over there.
Next to pretty and wanted,
And no need to be scared.
In the state of flawless
And the city of beautiful hair,
Lies a street they call skinny,
It's just over there.
Where they don't make themselves nauseous,
Or cry in a mirror.
They don't make their arms scarred,
Bodies sick, self-images bruised
Her life is simple, not terribly hard.
I'll show you the way,
And give you a key.
If you would leave me at perfection,
Where I can be free.

An Open Letter To Anorexia

Dear Ana,

There are so many places you can go and look for thinspiration, fitspo's, and bonespo's. There are so many workouts you can attempt to do to soothe your insatiable need for more. There is a never ending supply of water to replace all the foods you have restricted from your mouth. There are always new scales and body tape measures to give you numbers to frown upon. There will always be an entire land of struggling, battered, aching winter-girls stuck in the blinding blizzard of hunger, you among them. You always stand in front of the mirror beating yourself down until you are nothing more than a scared little girl hiding behind your porcelain bones constructed on a wire frame. You're so scared of the voices that made you want to tear yourself open to make them stop. You're scared of eating. And you feel next to nothing when you step on the scale. 128...125...119...116...112...107...105...99...95...92...87...83! You watch the numbers dwindle down with the hair falling out of your scalp. Never to be satisfied with the number on the scale, never to be enough. You have been blinded with the many pictures of skeletons made into gods and goddesses. You have been fooled with words like "thin", "pretty", and "'perfect". When all you can feel is your heavy heart weighing you down into the deepest debts of your seas of affliction. You can now only feel the curve of your hipbones, the bumps of your spine, and the rungs of your ribs where the body shaking pain crawls out to escape you. You run your fingers over them when you're praying for smaller jeans and to lose ten more pounds because you can't withstand the small bowl of tomato soup your mother forced down into your pink squeaky clean stomach. Because for you, your stomach grumbles are applauses for skipping so many meals and the blood that runs red from your arms and legs are worth every pound that you lose. But forget you Ana. forget you for withering away into nothing, and ruining the lives of those around you. Forget you for fooling me into thinking that I can never be enough until I end up like you, withered away into a big mess of nothing, with bones piled up on a hospital bed and scars running up and down my arms as I take heaving breaths to survive. Forget you for making me compulsively count my calories, saying I don't deserve to eat. Forget you for not letting me stop, no matter how many times I begged, and now I can't stop. We were the only people we had, you only had me and I only had you. The only thing we could hold onto. I was so stupid for letting me barricade me and trap me into a deteriorating downward spiral of self-inflicting harm and bitterness. I can't even begin to explain my disgust and fervid rancor for you and what you do, not just to me but to anyone who is vulnerable to fall for you and you toxic lies and tantalizing laughter. So Ana, tell me what it's like to be you. Tell me what it's like to ruin lives to the point where I don't have anything more to live for. Tell me what it's like when you twist the knife in someone's back. Tell me how you can sleep at night knowing you make me stand on that scale and taunt and ridicule the numbers that appear, as if I didn't already hate myself for eating. Tell me how you live with yourself knowing you're a cold blooded murderer.

You dug your own grave with a long handled spoon, the same spoon you were fed glass dreams with as a child; the glass dreams that ripped you from the inside out. You and I both know much too well how agonizing it is to be the daughter of parents who can't see you, not even when you're yelling and stomping in front of them. I know what it's like to drag that sharp object across your skin, because everything is too much, you feel too much, you think too much, everything is simply too much. And you don't know how to deal with it, no one ever taught you how to appreciate the air being exchanged in your lungs, no one ever taught you how to smile simply because you are happy. No one ever taught you what love was, and that is why you are the way you are. That is why you are Ana. And I know what triggers most of your life-threatening earthquakes. I am familiar with the demons inside of you; because once you were gone you left those to me in your will. They are the ones that I now battle against everyday. It's always a never ending battle for us, isn't it? And it's much too hard to look in the mirror without wanting to beat it to shards with your own two bony fists. It's much too hard to recover because everyone mocks our illness as if it were one of the funniest jokes. But we don't find any humor in it, but we never have the willpower to speak up because we spend all our strength on trying to ignore the hunger that slides its hands around my neck in a death-choke. It's much too hard to be in remission when you care too much about everything but care about nothing at all, when your sadness never leaves, when no one knows what you're dealing with because you won't let anyone in. It's so hard, and you don't want to do this anymore. Your eyes shone so bright Ana; I wish I could've saved your light instead of putting it out with my own. You lay to rest, because your lungs want an endless nap, and so does your weakened heart. You just want to be okay, so you lay to sleep without fear, and as you drift off into an addicting darkness, you know you have lost, and won only yourself the winter girl trip, too bad you were already hell bound.

You lost Ana, and I won.

The Scale

An obsession
An addiction
It tortures me,
But I need it.
I got to know
The number on the scale

Restrict my food
Eat
Purge
Thoughts of laxatives
My relationship with food.
It's unsafe
This is what happens.
I got to know
The number on the scale

I feel beautiful
Let me wear clothes that fit
I feel fat.
I'll wear clothes to hide my body
I got to know
The number on the scale

Just One Job...May Change My Life

Just one job may change my life. Involving a part of my past that haunts my days. To make this simpler let me rephrase. For twenty five years I have had this fear of eating food. From experience I know it can and will ruin your mood. Being social is a constant daily struggle. I feel like I have to live in my personal bubble. I do not want others to judge my behavior. So I avoid my friends, family, and my neighbors. My dream job would be helping others with eating issues or other mental health issues. Sitting there, listening, and handing them tissues. I know first-hand not wanting to eat. It is such a hard task to try to defeat. I want to help people overcome what I am working on overcoming from. I want to be the person they can call at 2am on the phone. My dream job would not only change my life but others too. Be there for people, and help them chew.

I'm Just Tired

I'm just tired.
I'm tired of turning on a TV that only shows me pictures
Of pretty girls, perfect girls, all a size double zero.
I'm tired of walking down the isle of my grocery store
Where magazines are advertising how to lose ten pounds
jump out at me.
I'm tired of turning on Facebook to ads that claim they have
Discovered fifteen foods that you should avoid at all costs to
slim down.
Slim down.
Lose weight.
Thigh gap.
Belly fat.
Diet. Diet. Diet.
I'm tired of the never ending stream of media on so subtly
Suggesting that we need to buy the next weight lose pill,
drink,
0-cal beverage, and try their new "skinny" program.
Because for some of us, for me, it's not all that subtle,
It's like screaming in my face
that I'm too fat to be in this world.
Like this world only has a place for the pretty girls.
The ones with the perfect bodies, perfect hair,
and perfect smile.
The ones that the men love because they look like they just
walked off a runway.
I'm tired.

Tired of wishing I was someone else, looked like
someone else,
And ate like someone else.
Tired of looking in the mirror and hating what I see and
knowing that I've tried it all,
That no matter how skinny I get I'll always look disgusting,
That I'll never look like the models on the screen
or the people around me.
I'm tired of knowing that large or small I still can't compete
And I'm always someone's second choice.
I'm tired of seeing the world like I do,
Because I don't see it like anyone else does.
I see people enjoying life and laughing and having fun and
I wish that was me.
I wish that I didn't have to take eighteen pills
A day to function the way that I should.
I hate that I got stuck with a disease that doesn't have a cure.
A disease that makes people look down on me
when they know.
Why couldn't I have gotten stuck with cancer?
At least you can treat it and it can be cured
so that it goes away.
At least it's possible.
At least cancer patients aren't looked down on.
That's one of the worst parts about it.
What I have to spend the rest of my life with is just as bad
And instead of people coming to you with their support and
Love they all run away and make fun of others who go
through the same thing.

Why can't they just understand that I hurt just as bad
or worse?
That it's like I have cancer everyday of my life and they can
never cure me.
That I just have to live through the pain every single day until
the day that I die.
It's not something that you can just tell people.
Not something that they understand.
They don't get how hard it can be to have your body not work
the way it should.
They expect you to just snap out of it or listen to what they
have to say
And decide that you are perfect the way that you are,
Just decide that everything is fine and dandy.
As if right after that you will always eat the perfect size meal
And never under-eat and life will move on.
But it's not like that.
It's not possible.
Not even after treatment.
It never goes away.
It never leaves.
Some days you just wish you could walk out into the street
And have a car hit you so you don't have to live
In a world that you don't fit into.
Other days you wish you would die so you don't have to fight
The urge to purge and wake up miserable
In your body and still other days you wish you would die
Just because you can't stand making yourself eat.
Most days I wish I would die period.
It's not that I'm suicidal, I'm just tired.

I'm tired of fighting.
I'm tired of fighting when I know I will always be
at a stalemate
With this disease where neither one of us can win.
I'm just tired.
And if I could change anything I would make it so
No one had to feel this feeling.
No one ever.

When I Go To Find Myself, I Know Where I'll Be

I'm finally going to fill up the pages of my life.
No more blanks. No more hesitation to fill in the spaces with bold, deliberate strokes.

I'm going to be able to focus again and spend my time thinking about the universe o more time, or circumstance, or existence; or really being with my friends and my family and my interactions will be whole and they'll be meaningful and I won't be sad that I can't give more.

I'm going to use my time to achieve and accomplish smaller things and bigger things and confidently conquer the world while working to get to where I want to be.

I'm not anxious, or self concerned, and my self consciousness doesn't make me want to shrink back and get quieter, paler, or remind me why I shouldn't be VIBRANT and proudly BE.

I want to exist with purpose that isn't destructive. I won't look at nature wistfully, but appreciatively, and I'll be able to accept, love, and spread that sense of wonder and contentment that comes with being happy just because I am a part of it. I won't begrudge myself happiness, or forever dwell on the errors and the wrongs and the mistakes that I've made and continue to let myself believe that I can't participate in the love and intimacy of truly knowing others.

I will be so much a part of my life. I will learn what true fullness is and I will cry at the magnitudes, significance, awesomeness, sincerity, profundity, beauty, and absoluteness of this feeling that has eluded me this whole time.

I will be brave in the face of my doubts, and I will be stronger for others. I will live the life that I have wanted for myself all along, without being distracted by my fears, or deterring myself in the belief that I cannot and am not enough.

I am going to feel so much.

And I will do other things, seemingly insignificant, like eating a bowl of cereal. I will mean it when I say that I don't want any, because it will no longer come from a place of doubt and insecurity.

I will trust and invest in myself and in others. I will allow myself to really feel, and the connections may be fleeting, but they will be authentic.

I think it would be lovely, really, tragically beautiful, to be able to cry, be upset, or be angry without feeling more responsible to others than to myself.

I will use my true voice and I will be amused, consumed, entrenched, engulfed, and enraptured by my fear, excitement, empathy, happiness, confusion, and frustration when I feel and know myself again.

I will learn for the very, very first time who I am without Anorexia and Bulimia and this perpetual sense of shame and it will be like stepping into the sunshine and finally meeting true warmth.

I am excited to get to know myself again. I am sad for the time that I have lost and the self that I've lost. But I won't always be sad about that.

I know that, more than anything I will be grateful to have experienced so much pain, sadness, numbness, fear, worry, hardship, shame, guilt, and embarrassment because it has allowed me to, forced me to find myself.

And for the first time also, those that I know and love and those that I don't know yet will have a chance to finally see all of me and to truly know me; even and especially the parts that I'm afraid of letting anyone see.

Trusting myself, and trusting others and knowing that we are all trying our hardest to be who and what and how we want to be and knowing that we will all come up short sometimes will be reassurance that we are all, finally human.

I will love myself despite my flaws, and maybe I will even revel in them because THESE are the things that make me quintessentially myself.

No. I won't define myself in such lines and terms and set

expectations that I don't understand or find achievable. I will live day by day, and I will make the best of it; but I will no longer terrorize myself or hurt myself or see the reflection of my failures in vomit.

Skinny, Pretty, Dead

It's 11:43pm and all I can hear is the voices in my head silently screaming at me about all the calories that I've eaten today. I tell myself I need to be things that I am not, I tell myself that I need to be three things that I am not, I tell myself that I need to be three things that I am not so that I may be loved, so that I may be cared about. I tell myself that I must be these three things; Skinny, Pretty, Dead, Skinny, Pretty, Dead. I must be these three things to make the world a better place. I must be skinny so that I don't take up too much space, I must be pretty so that I am not a thing that is torture to those who are forced to lay their eyes upon, and I must be dead so I don't screw up anymore than I have, to finally be gone. Skinny, Pretty, Dead, Skinny, Pretty, Dead, the three things that constantly run through my head. Skinny. Pretty. Dead.

The Beast Behind The Beauty

Why does she stand alone?
Why does she shy away from those who care most?
Why is the damsel in distress, still in distress?
Why does she stand alone?

How often does she wish that she were someone else?
How many times has she rejected genuine compliments?
How long does she spend concealing, contouring, lightening,
and brightening her flawless face?
How often does she wish that she were someone else?

Who told her that she was not enough?
Who kicked her back down just as
She built the courage to stand up?
Who closed the door as she knocked frantically?
Who told her that she was not enough?

It is the beast behind beauty.
The pain behind the smile.
The brokenness among the laughter.
And the confidence that couldn't ever reach a mile.

It is the beast behind beauty.
Where she couldn't bear to say
"I am alright and I am okay"

It is the beast behind beauty.
And the beauty swallowed her whole.

Approval

I've decided to eat today…
Is a cup of coffee okay?
Only if it's black,
Maybe some cherries?
Only three allowed for you,
Okay…what about some chicken?
You're really pushing it,
Okay, okay, maybe just one key lime pie…
No no just one small slice I mean,
Can;t believe you even considered that…
Sorry,
Just for that you deserve nothing,
Okay,
I guess I won't be eating today.

About The Author

As a young teen, Misty Hicks began to believe the lies she was being told by others. You're getting fat. That ice cream will make you bloat. You're too short to ever be skinny. As she drew the conclusion that she would never be thin enough to look good or measure up to other girls, she turned her feelings inward, began to skip meals, purge, take laxatives, and over exercise. Whatever it took, she wanted to prove them wrong.

Now an adult, with a teen girl of her own, Misty is facing the effects of a long term eating disorder. Damaged has been done to nearly every part of her body due to malnutrition. While she is on her journey of healing, Misty has tapped into her creative outlet of writing to give expression to her thoughts and feelings. Her hope is that the poems you hold in your hand will bring better understanding and a sense of hope if you struggle with an eating disorder or know someone who does.

Misty is also the author of *Beyond Abuse: Moving Forward One Day At A Time*. Along with writing, she enjoys being a mom of five, painting, and being active in her church.

www.ingramcontent.com/pod-product-compliance
Lightning Source LLC
Chambersburg PA
CBHW022016290426
44109CB00015B/1197